Alvin ISD
Bel Nafegar Sanchez Elementary School
1721 Sterling Lakes West Drive
Rosharon, TX 77583

September 11 and Terrorism in America

A MODERN PERSPECTIVES BOOK

Tamra B. Orr

Published in the United States of America by Cherry Lake Publishing
Ann Arbor, Michigan
www.cherrylakepublishing.com

Content Adviser: Satta Sarmah Hightower, Writer & Editor, Talented Tenth Media, Boston, MA
Reading Adviser: Marla Conn MS, Ed., Literacy specialist, Read-Ability, Inc.

Photo Credits: © Joseph Sohm / Shutterstock.com, cover, 1, 5, 12; © Kdonmuang / Shutterstock.
com, 4; © lebedev / Shutterstock.com, 7; © Robert Hoetink / Shutterstock.com, 9; © NAPI WAN
ALI / Shutterstock.com, 10; © Azovtsev Maksym / Shutterstock.com, 11; © Jonathan Feinstein /
Shutterstock.com, 14; © Victor Moussa / Shutterstock.com, 15; © LAURA SALERI /
Shutterstock.com, 17; © Kotsovolos Panagiotis / Shutterstock.com, 19, 30; © Africa Studio /
Shutterstock.com, 22; © Asianet-Pakistan / Shutterstock.com, 23; © Michael Heimlich /
Shutterstock.com, 25; © Evan El-Amin / Shutterstock.com, 29

Graphic Element Credits: ©RoyStudioEU/Shutterstock.com, back cover, front cover, multiple
interior pages; ©queezz/Shutterstock.com, back cover, front cover, multiple interior pages

Library of Congress Cataloging-in-Publication Data
Names: Orr, Tamra B., author.
Title: September 11 and terrorism in America / Tamra B. Orr.
Description: Ann Arbor : Cherry Lake Publishing, 2017. | Series: Modern perspectives | Includes
    bibliographical references and index.
Identifiers: LCCN 2016058625| ISBN 9781634728584 (hardcover) | ISBN 9781534100367
    (paperback) | ISBN 9781634729475 (PDF) | ISBN 9781534101258 (hosted ebook)
Subjects: LCSH: September 11 Terrorist Attacks, 2001—Juvenile literature. | September 11 Terrorist
    Attacks, 2001—Biography—Juvenile literature. | Muslim students—New York (State)—New
    York—Biography—Juvenile literature. | Fire fighters—New York (State)—New York—
    Biography—Juvenile literature. | Students—Middle West—Biography—Juvenile literature.
Classification: LCC HV6432.7 .O79 2017 | DDC 974.7/10440922—dc23
LC record available at https://lccn.loc.gov/2016058625

Cherry Lake Publishing would like to acknowledge the work of
The Partnership for 21st Century Skills. Please visit *www.p21.org*
for more information.

Printed in the United States of America
Corporate Graphics

Table of Contents

In this book, you will read three different perspectives about the terrorist attacks in New York City on September 11, 2001. While these characters are fictionalized, each perspective is based on real things that happened to real people during and after the attacks. As you'll see, the same event can look different depending on one's point of view.

Chapter 1

Amna Nasir

New York Muslim Student

I pulled my **hijab** closer around my face and kept my eyes down as I walked over to my bus. I dreaded the trip home from school every single day. Ever since the Twin Towers were attacked in New York City a month ago, the 30-minute trip from school to my block felt like forever. It seemed like suddenly, instead of just being an eighth-grade student who loved science, was allergic to cats, and lived on Morrison Street, I was a target. Thanks to Osama bin Laden and the **extremist** group Al-Qaeda claiming responsibility for the attacks on 9/11, all Muslims—including my family—became national enemies.

▲ *The Twin Towers were a part of the World Trade Center in New York City. When the towers were dedicated, in 1973, they were the tallest buildings in the world.*

"Hey, Muslim girl," shouted a boy two rows behind me. "What are you going to blow up next?" I sat up straighter and looked out the window, pretending I hadn't heard him. I could feel my cheeks get hot and knew I was blushing.

"Yeah, Amna," said a girl in front of me who had turned around to glare. "Why don't you just go back to where you came from and leave Americans alone?"

It wasn't fair. I was an American! I had lived in the United States my entire life. My parents came here from Afghanistan years before I was born. My brother, Asir, was just a little baby then. We had nothing at all to do with what happened to the World Trade Center, but anyone following our religion of Islam was being held responsible

Second Source

▶ Find a second source that describes what the religion of Islam is about. Compare the information there to the information in this book.

▲ *Afghanistan is a country in the Middle East that has endured many years of war and fighting.*

Think About It

▶ Read the paragraph about the discrimination that Amna's family had experienced. What is the main point of this paragraph? Pick out one piece of evidence that supports the main point.

for the horrible attacks. Nearly 3,000 people had lost their lives as airplanes were used as weapons of mass murder. Asir and I watched the news reports every day for weeks and were horrified at what we saw. My parents immediately went down to the closest Red Cross and stood in line for hours to donate blood. We all went to our **mosque** to pray, and we returned several times to help box up supplies and food for the rescue workers who were helping at Ground Zero.

"Did you hear?" shouted a boy in the next row. "Science flies you to the moon, but Muslims just fly you into buildings." Everyone laughed, but I was shocked. Not only was it an ignorant and unkind comment, but 9/11 was nothing anyone should joke about.

Of course, it was not just me who was experiencing these reactions. My whole family had suffered from some type of religious

discrimination since the attacks. My cousin Tamir had been fired from his job without warning after 9/11. My uncle Zayan was thrown out of a grocery store when he tried to do his regular shopping there. My aunt Mimra's dry-cleaning business lost more than half of its customers without any explanation. My brother had

▲ *Those responsible for the attacks on September 11, 2001, were religious extremists. They had very little in common with Muslims.*

▲ *Muslims worship at a mosque. Many mosques in America were vandalized after the attack on the World Trade Center.*

been kicked off of his high school's football team, even though he was one of the best quarterbacks the school had ever had. I could not think of anyone in my family who had not felt the impact of history's biggest and most brutal attack. On top of that, our mosque's windows had been broken by people throwing rocks in the middle of the night.

As I climbed off the bus, someone threw out one more remark. "Take your religion of hate and go back to Iraq!"

I could only shake my head. I wasn't from Iraq, and Islam is not a religion of hate, but of peace. Millions of people followed Islam in the

▲ *Many Muslim families were unable to go about their daily life without harassment.*

▲ *President George W. Bush led the country after the attacks. Many Americans were very scared.*

United States and were not violent. I closed my eyes and remembered the words of President Bush a few days after the towers were destroyed. "The face of terror is not the true faith of Islam," he stated in a speech at the Islamic Center of Washington, D.C. "That's not what Islam is all about. Islam is peace. These **terrorists** don't represent peace. They represent evil and war."

Now if only my classmates—and so many others—would just listen. I am a friend and an American, not a terrorist or an enemy.

Pillars of a Faith

The Five Tenets of Islam, also known as the Five Pillars, are the primary duties that every Muslim is to perform during his or her lifetime. These core beliefs include a declaration of faith, daily prayer, freely giving to others, fasting at set times of the year, and traveling to Mecca, a holy destination.

Chapter 2

Marcus Cooper

NYFD Firefighter

I woke up yelling in the darkness, trying to find my way out of the nightmare I was having. As usual, I had dreamt I was at the World Trade Center. I was somewhere near the 60th floor and trying to make my way down the stairs with a wounded man over my right shoulder. In the dream, the stairs never ended. I just kept going down farther and farther, surrounded by thick smoke and the cries of people who needed my help. I always woke before I found a way out.

I got out of bed and went into the kitchen to relive the memories and then try to let them go. As one of the hundreds of firefighters

▲ *New York City firefighters were among the very first rescue workers to respond the morning of September 11, 2001.*

who had rushed to the site of 9/11 weeks ago, I was sure I wasn't the only one having frequent nightmares. I always slept with the lights on now, because the dark was too thick with memories.

I had wanted to be a firefighter for as long as I could remember. When I was little, I always watched the TV show *Emergency*. It was my favorite show. I wanted to wear the protective fire gear and ride in the fire truck, sirens blaring. I couldn't wait to grow up and learn how to rescue people from burning buildings.

After 10 years as a firefighter, I still loved my job, but I could never have imagined what would happen on September 11, 2001. I was on duty that morning when the alarms in the firehouse began screaming. Right away, we knew this was not the usual house on fire.

Second Source

▶ Find a second source that details the different types of responders who were at Ground Zero. How does the information from that source compare to the information here?

Fire departments from all five of New York City's **boroughs** were being called in: Queens, Brooklyn, Staten Island, the Bronx, and ours, in Manhattan. We were told that a plane had hit the North Tower of the World Trade Center between floors 94 and 99. As we made our way through traffic, we heard the second tower had just been hit between the 78th and 84th floors. We knew that each of those planes was full of thousands of gallons of fuel. The idea that

▲ In 2006, a memorial wall was built to honor the 343 firefighters who lost their lives.

Analyze This

▶ Why would outdated radios make a disaster like 9/11 even more difficult to handle? Give two reasons for your answer.

these planes had been used deliberately was something none of us could believe.

When we reached the World Trade Center, the place was total chaos. Both of the towers had collapsed, and the air was filled with dust, smoke, and debris, blocking the sun. The towers looked like skeletons, and people were screaming and running away as fast as possible. As a first responder, I did what we were trained to do—run toward the danger, not away from it. One volunteer fireman I met described it this way: "Those of us who wear uniforms make a living out of the worst 10 minutes of everybody's lives."

The next few hours of my life were the most challenging I've ever experienced. The people I rescued—and those I tried to rescue but failed—now fill my nightmares. Our radios, which were **outdated** and unreliable even during the 1990s, were real problems during this chaos. We couldn't get messages in or out. So we had no way of talking to commanders or asking whether we should be evacuating people or searching for those on the upper floors. By then we had been told of the other two flights that had crashed, including one at the Pentagon near Washington, D.C., and one in a field outside Shanksville, Pennsylvania.

Now, weeks later, I sat back in my chair and took a few deep breaths. The horror of 9/11 was still fresh in my mind. I had been back countless times to work on **The Pile**, and it was always

▲ *Some of the wreckage from the towers is on display at the 9/11 Memorial and Museum in New York City.*

Flight Information	Civilian Deaths	Terrorists
American Airlines 767 Flight 11 Boston, MA, to Los Angeles, CA	92	5
United Airlines 767 Flight 175 Boston, MA, to Los Angeles, CA	65	5
American Airlines 757 Flight 77 Washington, DC, to Los Angeles, CA	64	5
United Airlines 757 Flight 93 Newark, NJ, to San Francisco, CA	40	4

discouraging. It was a six-story-tall pile of rubble that shifted every time you took a step.

Hundreds and hundreds of police officers, firefighters, and emergency medical workers were there alongside me, hour after hour. There were hundreds of volunteers, too—everyday people who wanted to help. Red Cross members were handing out bottles of water. The nation really pulled together during these dark, dark days. As President Bush told the country, "Today, our nation saw evil, the very worst of human nature, and we responded with the best of America, with the daring of our rescue workers, with the caring for strangers and neighbors who came to give blood and help in any way they could."

Why some terrorists in the Middle East wanted to hurt so many innocent people is more than I can begin to understand. Thousands died that day, including people in the towers, airline passengers, and first responders. I lost some of my closest friends, along with my sister-in-law and uncle. It is little wonder I still have nightmares. Life will never be the same for me—or for any American.

Chapter 3

Jeremy Loomis
Michigan Student

"**Y**ou heard the president," said my father as he sat down at the dining room table. "He said it clear. 'Make no mistake, the United States will hunt down and punish those responsible for these cowardly attacks.' See? He is telling us that we have to go to war." Dad added, "It's time for revenge for what was done to our country!"

I stood in the hallway, listening to my parents. Ever since the World Trade Center was attacked a month ago, all my parents talked about was who was responsible and what role the Muslims had in it. I was confused. I thought the person behind the 9/11 attacks was someone named Osama bin Laden. I heard in school that he and his

▲ *Osama bin Laden was the extremist who organized the attacks on America.*

group of followers, Al-Qaeda, believed in an extreme version of Islam that said Muslims should attack anyone who didn't agree with their religion. My best friend Chin's parents said that bin Laden called Americans **infidels**. They said bin Laden told his people that killing enemies was holy work. The news stated that he convinced the hijackers they were heroes and would be awarded with life in paradise for their acts.

But I know several Muslims at school, and they do not seem angry or scary. Zayam sits next to me in math, and he is always making jokes. Aleena has a locker next to mine, and she has the sweetest smile.

"Dad," I asked, walking into the kitchen, "what do you really think we should do about the attacks?"

▲ *After the September 11 attacks, many Americans showed their solidarity with the rest of the country by hanging American flags.*

My dad looked guilty for a moment, but then answered. "What was done to our country is unforgivable, son," he said. "Even the president has said we have to find the people behind the evil acts and bring them to justice!"

"But the president meant just the terrorists—Osama bin Laden and Al-Qaeda," I explained. "In his speech just a few days after 9/11, he said that Muslims should be treated with respect. I have Muslim friends at school. Some of the kids have been really mean to them."

"They're frightened, and they're angry, Jeremy," my mother said. "Something terrible happened to the United States, and thousands lost their lives. Many people—young and old—don't know what to do with those feelings, so they end up lashing out."

She glanced over at Dad, and he slowly nodded his head. "You're both right," he said. "Jeremy, maybe we should do something to help those friends of yours. Give it some thought."

"But not now," Mom said with a smile. "It's time for bed."

As I lay in bed that night, my mind was busy. Wasn't there something I could do? By Saturday morning, I had an idea. For my birthday, I had gotten a button maker. I hadn't done much with it yet, but now I had a purpose for it. I came up with just the right words to put on a button. While I was making the buttons, my dad stopped by to

Remembering Loss

During a memorial service in 2011, New York mayor Michael Bloomberg addressed a nation that still remembered its losses. The mayor stated, "Ten years have passed since a perfect blue sky morning turned into the blackest of nights. Since then we've lived in sunshine and in shadow, and although we can never unsee what happened here, we can also see that children who lost their parents have grown into young adults, grandchildren have been born, and good works and public service have taken root to honor those we loved and lost."

Think About It

▶ Read the ending of the chapter. How did Mr. Loomis's opinion change from the beginning of the chapter? Why do you think he changed his mind?

help me. I went to school with enough buttons for my entire class. With my teacher's permission, I handed them out.

The buttons stated, "Never forget: We're all in this together." They were a reminder that we were united in our feelings, not divided. When I handed a button to Aleena, she gave me the sweetest smile of all. The other kids in class asked if I could make more for them to hand out. Of course, I said yes!

That night, when Dad came home from work, I saw he had a button pinned to his jacket. I told him I needed to make more for my friends at school, and he chuckled. "People at work are asking for some, too," he said. "So, let's get to work."

▲ *The monument in New York City sometimes shines lights into the night sky where the Twin Towers used to stand.*

Look, Look Again

Take a look at this photo from the 9/11 Memorial and Museum in New York City. Use the photograph to help you answer the following questions:

1. How would a Muslim student feel about this picture? How might she explain September 11 to a friend?

2. How do you think a New York firefighter might react to this photo? Do you think his reaction would be the same as a firefighter from a different state?

3. What would a family who had never seen the World Trade Center think about this photo? How might that be different than a family who had visited recently?

Glossary

boroughs (BUR-ohz) governmental and geographical divisions of New York City

discrimination (dis-krim-ih-NAY-shuhn) the act of treating a person differently based on that person's race, gender, or age

extremist (ik-STREE-mist) a person who supports a cause to extreme measures

hijab (he-JAHB) the traditional covering for the hair and neck worn by Muslim women

infidels (IN-fih-delz) people who do not accept a particular faith

mosque (MAHSK) a Muslim temple or place of worship

outdated (out-DAY-tid) no longer current or modern

terrorists (TER-ur-ists) people who frighten others, often violently

The Pile (THUH PILE) the rescue workers' nickname for Ground Zero

Learn More

Further Reading

Baskin, Nora Raleigh. *Nine, Ten: A September 11 Story*. New York: Atheneum Books for Young Readers, 2016.

Murray, Laura K. *The 9/11 Terror Attacks*. Mankato, MN: Creative Education, 2016.

Rhodes, Jewell Parker. *Towers Falling*. New York: Little Brown and Company, 2016.

Tarshis, Lauren. *I Survived the Attacks of September 11, 2001*. New York: Scholastic Press, 2012.

Zullo, Allan. *Heroes of 9/11*. New York: Scholastic, 2011.

Web Sites

Ducksters—US History: September 11 Attacks
www.ducksters.com/history/us_1900s/september_11_attacks.php

Scholastic—What Happened on 9/11?
www.scholastic.com/browse/article.jsp?id=3756477

Index

About the Author

Tamra Orr clearly remembers 9/11 and the pain that the nation and its people suffered from it. She is the author of hundreds of books for readers of all ages. She lives in the Pacific Northwest with her family and spends all of her free time writing letters, reading books, and going camping. She graduated from Ball State University with a degree in English and education, and believes she has the best job in the world. It gives her the chance to keep learning all about the world and the people in it.